FALL IN LOVE WITH YOUR FUTURE

EXPLORING THE PATH TO A MEANINGFUL LIFE

MARY & RON BESHEAR

This motivational book is written with the desire that every reader find encouragement for overcoming personal setbacks and living out his or her best destiny. Few things are more fulfilling than understanding one's own unique potential and using personal energy on things of lasting value.

Fall in Love with your Future was born out of the authors' belief that everyone has an infinite capacity to impact the world for good.

Fall in Love with Your Future

© 1999 by Mary and Ron Beshear

Revised, 2011

ISBN: 1460951204
ISBN-13: 9781460951200

THEMES

FALL IN LOVE WITH YOUR FUTURE

EXPLORING THE PATH TO A MEANINGFUL LIFE

Mary and Ron Beshear

We all make mistakes and experience disappointment. Sometimes our biggest regret is that we can't undo the past. It's like concrete that has hardened and can't be reshaped.

That's why the future offers such hope. No matter how old we are, each new day stretches before us like wet cement . . . waiting for the imprint we give it. Wise daily decisions can help us build more of the things we truly desire: nobility of character, revived relationships, even increased personal power.

This book describes the kind of decisions and life-skills that lead to purpose and contentment. Practicing these skills frees us to catch a glimpse of who we really are and the destiny that is open to us. Once we understand and fall in love with our future, it's possible that the world around us will never be the same.

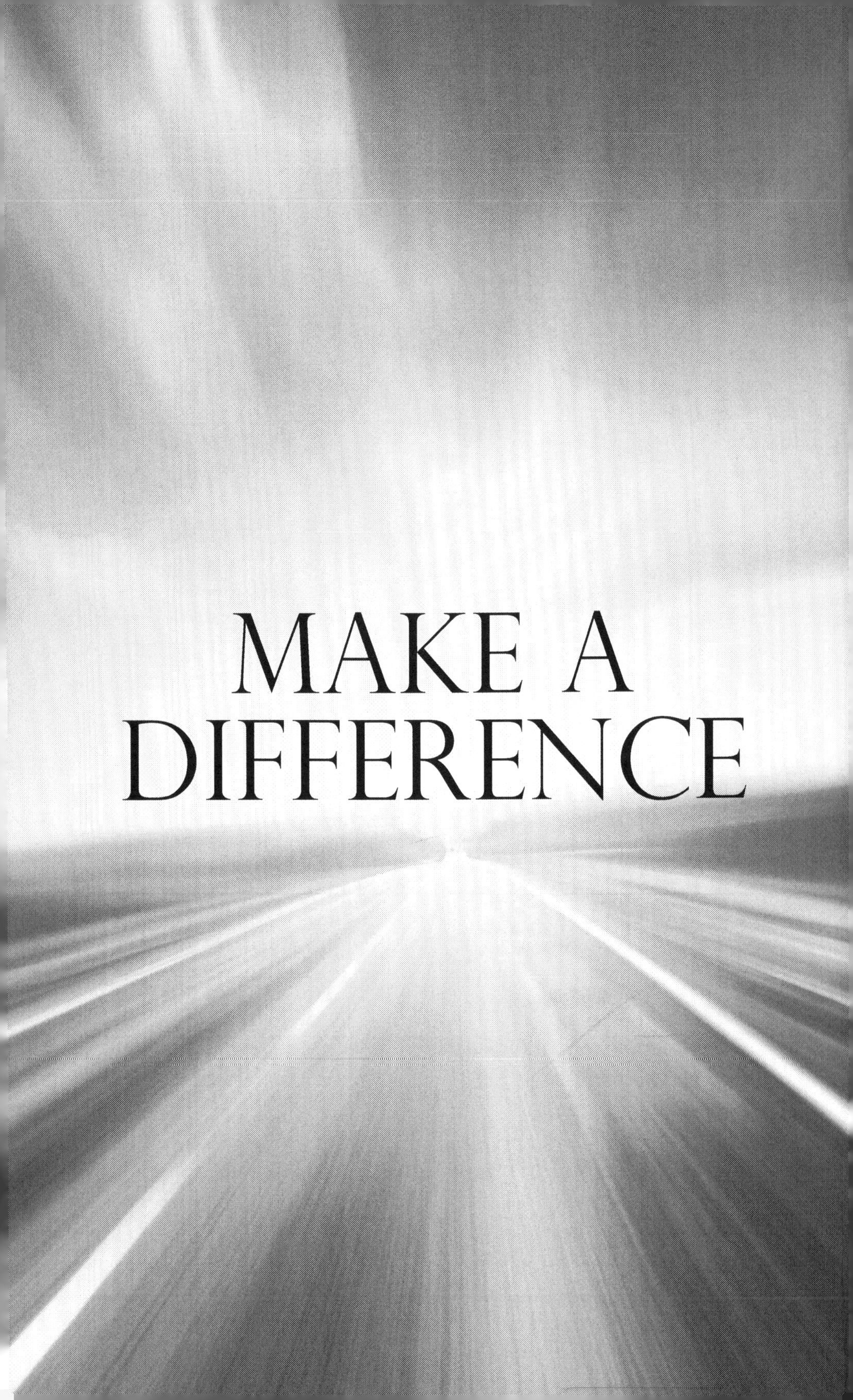
MAKE A
DIFFERENCE

A consultant who traveled to over 100 different countries through his professional assignments kept a private survey of questions he asked in his spare time. One of the questions was, "What's the most important thing in life to you?" The answer he received over and over was, "I want my life to count."

Another question he asked was, "What is your greatest fear?" Surprisingly, very few people said things like death, cancer, or public humiliation. Instead, most confided a fear that their lives would be meaningless—that they would die with their potential untapped.

When pressed, most of us feel there's a reason we were put on Earth at this place and time. We have an inner longing to fulfill that destiny, even if we don't know exactly what it is. And we don't have to know. Rick Warren, author of *The Purpose Driven Life*, says that "anytime we use our God- given abilities to help others, we *are* fulfilling our calling."

Getting excited about our future prompts us to go beyond simply surviving. In fact, it actually prompts us to go beyond seeking success. Ultimately, it motivates us to look for significance, which involves finding ways to fulfill a purpose greater than ourselves.

People who have fallen in love with their future have usually discovered this value of being other-centered. And they apply it to their careers, as well as to their personal lives. They try to look 5, 10, 20 years into the future and ask themselves, "Is what I'm doing benefitting mankind?" "Will it continue to serve others in the future?" If not, they do the soul searching necessary for a career or personal change. If so, they throw themselves into their work with a new vision for making a difference.

"We each have a song within us that only we can sing."
Michael Jones

DEVELOP A VISION THAT FITS YOU

Looking at the future with new eyes can be intimidating. It might lead someone to reevaluate a career that has brought success but no joy. Or prompt another to pursue more training. However, reevaluation can lead to change and therefore risk.

The key is to develop a vision that fits your unique strengths and gifts. A future that reflects your passion. Ask yourself, "What would I do if there were no risk of failure?" "What would I keep doing even if I were not paid for the work?" "What is one task that causes me to lose track of time when I'm doing it?"

If you can't decide whether to call an activity 'work' or 'play,' your enjoyment for the task will empower achievement and enrich your life far beyond reputation or salary. Radio life-coach, John Tesh, puts it another way. He says, "Our deepest desire will eventually seek its rightful place in our lives. Like a bottle of cola forgotten in the freezer, there *will* be an explosion. It's only a matter of time."

That colorful metaphor reminds us it's wise to think about things we enjoy doing, tasks we do well, and personal work others have noticed. A good mentor will then advise:

- dream, pray, and look for a vision,
- take stock of your resources and acquire any needed training,
- develop an action plan with specific goals and deadlines, and
- modify your plan as you go along.

Someone once said we should look at our talents, then envision the future adorned with them. Our future is as personal and unique as our own fingerprint. It is energizing to recognize and use our true talents generously. As we do, the future can, indeed, be faced with great anticipation!

"My object in living is to unite my avocation with my vocation."
Robert Frost

LOOK WHERE YOU WANT TO GO

W hat sets apart those who have an exciting future from those who are barely getting by? Men and women who have fallen in love with their future have discovered a profound principle. It's simply to choose a good plan and focus on it.

Have you ever watched a cat jump from a sitting position to a surface 15 times his height above him? He begins by looking around for a spot that interests him and then focusing on where he wants to go.

Race car drivers tell us that the way they get through a tight line of cars and seldom hit anything is that they focus on where they want to go. They train themselves not to look at the wall or at any obstacle they want to avoid, but to focus on the open space they want to fill.

What's the open space you want to fill? If it's legal, moral, and honorable, focus on it. Too often we spend our energy contemplating the things we want to avoid, rather than preparing for the things we want to accomplish. Shifting our focus from worry to action frees us to soar.

Look for an opportunity that fits your unique gifts, one that offers excellence and quality. Then focus on it and advance confidently in the direction of your goal.

"People with goals succeed because they know where they are going."
Earl Nightingale

STRETCH YOURSELF NOW TO SOAR LATER

Ours is a dynamic culture. Information, equipment, and career demands seem to change constantly. As a result, corporate leaders say the most important credentials men and women today can have for employment are personal resilience and a zeal for life-long learning.

Actually, those are qualities that also help a person remain excited about his or her future. The happiest people are those who continually work to improve their minds and grow in integrity and character.

If we read good books, choose heroic models, associate with virtuous people, and train ourselves to do even the smallest things with excellence, we open the door to greater prospects. Success is little more than the daily practice of simple disciplines.

On the other hand, expediencies that shortcut growth and learning often lead to disappointing outcomes. So we are wise to absorb all we can along the way and stretch ourselves to be the best we can be. Personal development is the most important credential for a dynamic future.

"Don't join an easy crowd," author Jim Rohn advises his counselees. "You won't grow. Go where the expectation and demands to perform are high." Then regularly ask yourself, "Who am I associating with? What have they got me reading, . . . thinking, . . . saying, . . .doing?" In short, "What have they got me becoming?"

These are smart questions. What we become in thought, heart, and spirit determines not only the direction of our forward motion, but also the height to which we can soar.

"The highest qualities of character . . . must be earned."
Lyman Abbott

THINK FEEDBACK, NOT FAILURE

The only people who never fail are those in cemeteries. It's not what happens in life that brings failure or success. It's how we perceive our circumstances and what we do about them.

Noted motivational speaker, Anthony Robbins, says "Winners, leaders, and masters all understand that if you try something and do not get the outcome you want, it's simply feedback."

Yet, if we don't monitor our thought life, every unintended error and every misjudgment takes on emotional significance. We begin to see human mistakes as personal failure and as a reflection on our character or reputation.

However, people who are ready to fall in love with their future are willing to view disappointing outcomes as feedback, not failure. They consciously work against letting emotional disappointment weigh them down. Instead, they focus on using the information to help them make finer distinctions about future action. Best selling author and motivational speaker Ken Blanchard puts it well when he says, "Feedback is the breakfast of champions."

Today, let's make a commitment to stop thinking in terms of failure; rather, let's think in terms of results. If we don't get the outcome we wanted, we need only change our actions to yield a new result over time. As we fall in love with our future, we commit to learning from every experience.

"When I have decided a result is worth getting, I go ahead on it and make trial after trial until it comes."
Thomas A. Edison

ENJOY THE REWARDS OF PLANNING

T he story is told of a young man who decided to climb the ladder of success. He put in long hours, sacrificed Saturdays with his family, and eventually inched his way up to the top rung on the corporate ladder—only to find that his ladder was against the wrong wall. The corner office on the executive floor did not satisfy his heart and spirit.

Personal soul-searching revealed that more balance between career and family was a better plan. In fact, this particular young man began to view life like a pentathlon, with a need to devote his energy and attention to five areas:

- career,
- family,
- faith,
- community, and
- personal health.

Each night, he made a list of the steps he could take the next day to nurture faith and family relationships. He wrote these in his daily planner alongside his professional tasks. Weekly or monthly, he checked his attention to health, as well as community contributions.

He realized that different stages of life sometimes called for more attention in one area than another, but his general quest was for balance in these areas. Once he determined what he wanted for his future and where he wanted his ladder, the daily climb was smoother.

Falling in love with your future means having a plan that gives you something to reach for. It's like have a north star to navigate by when life's undercurrents surprise you. Planning is the golden bridge to the future we desire.

"Most people plan their vacations with better care than they do their lives. Perhaps that is because escape is easier than change."

Jim Rohn

DON'T LET DISASTER KEEP YOU DOWN

Someone once made the point that it's a bad idea to become accustomed to good luck. Risk of disaster is part of life. A child dies as a result of e-coli infected water at an amusement park. An earthquake wipes out an entire city, leaving thousands homeless, without power, and grieving lost loved ones.

Sometimes tragedy strikes out of the blue. Sometimes it comes with advance warnings. Either way it usually knocks us breathless, whether it happens to us, to a friend, or to perfect strangers.

In spite of the heartache and scars, many 2005 Hurricane Katrina victims reported that adversity has one powerful advantage. It takes away all non-essentials and gives us no recourse but to rely on God and on our God- given strengths. It forces us to look at our core values.

After disaster, we often get sympathy and some kind of help for our misfortune. This is comforting for a while. Then at some point, the compassion fails to nourish and we realize there is no release from the weight of calamity until we take action ourselves. The action might involve finding a healthy way to work through the grief. It might involve forgiveness. It might involve rebuilding or laboring toward a change.

Jan Scruggs, a Vietnam veteran who lost his best friends in combat, decided to build the Vietnam Memorial as a testament to soldiers who gave up their lives in the war. Talking about Vietnam was not popular in 1980, but he knew the war experience needed to be healed—not forgotten. In the process of standing firm in his resolve, Scruggs broke through what the disaster had done to his psyche and fell in love with his future again.

We <u>can</u> go beyond disaster. The key is to revisit our core values and then go to work on a goal that touches head, heart, and spirit.

EXERCISE PERSONAL POWER

We give up personal power when we worry about popular opinion, let other people speak for us, or tell ourselves that others have more right to their preferences than we do. When we hold one of these attitudes, we subtly give those around us the power to dismiss our ideas or have *their* agenda worked out, possibly at *our* expense.

The people who are most excited about their future are those who exercise their own personal power. They believe they have the ability to evaluate, to make good choices, and to make worthy contributions. They put aside personal insecurities. They cheerfully ask for what they need and express gracious appreciation when they receive it. They thoughtfully offer creative ideas and personal opinions.

If it's true that most of us invent and live out self-fulfilling prophecies, we'd be wise to start each day by taking a realistic view of our God-given worth and talents. What responsibilities do these carry? What detrimental habits do we need to break so we can live out a prophecy more like the one for which we were born?

The truth is, no matter what our title or status, we have:

- the power to choose our attitude and our values,
- the right to say "no" to unreasonable demands, and
- the responsibility to avoid self defeating pursuits.

The greatest future in the world can look bleak when we have a victim mentality. But even the bleakest future has hope and dignity when we reclaim the power to make healthy choices and act on them.

"Man must cease attributing his problems to his environment and learn again to exercise his personal responsibility."
Albert Schweitzer

WORK ON YOUR
YOUR
BEST NATURAL
RESOURCE:
YOUR BODY

We may think that things like daily exercise, healthy eating habits, and adequate rest don't make a big difference, but the impact is long term and cumulative, rather than immediate.

An evergreen tree in our backyard developed a brown tinge in its branch tips. Then the branches began to dry and die. A horticulturist came to look for insect and root damage, but found none. Noting the tree's proximity to our swimming pool, he asked if the pool might have a leak. "No," I said, "but every few weeks when I backwash the pool filter, quite a bit of the pool water does spill under that tree."

"That's the problem!" he said confidently. "The salt in chlorine will kill just about any kind of plant." Unconvinced, I protested, "But I've been doing that for years and we've never had a problem before."

He looked at me squarely so his words would sink in. Then he said, "Ma'am, don't you know that the effect of harmful input is cumulative?"

Ultimately, we changed the soil around the tree, fertilized it with good nutrients, and rerouted our backwash device. Now the tree is vital and flourishing again.

Like the tree, our bodies are living things that need the right nourishment. Everything we eat and drink affects our cellular development. However, the discernable effect is cumulative, rather than immediate.

If you want to look forward to getting up in the mornings, rid yourself of anything that may be slowing you down or setting disease in process. Exercise regularly and take in only what will have a good cumulative effect. All our todays and tomorrows will be better when we feel healthy.

"The first wealth is health."
Ralph Waldo Emerson

RECOGNIZE THE POWER OF WORDS

Thoughts have tremendous power, and thoughts are triggered by words. Author and speaker, Les Brown, tells the story of a teacher who asked him to write something on the board. Brown, an 11th grader at the time, refused and said, "I can't, Sir; I'm educable mentally retarded."

The teacher's response changed Brown's life when he challenged him to be careful about the power that words and labels could have on him. His instructor said, "If you can get a glimpse of yourself, of who you really are, and what it is you bring to the planet in a historical sense, the world will never be the same."

Letting words be our tools, never our stumbling blocks, is a message we all could use. Medical science offers evidence that peaceful affirming words can lower blood pressure, reduce stress levels, and—in some cases—promote inexplicable physical healing.

Author and consultant, Steven Covey, gives some helpful advice on using words to reduce stress and promote honest exchanges. He says:

- prepare your heart and mind before you prepare your words,
- assume the best in others and let your words reflect that,
- refrain from saying the unkind or negative thing, especially when tired or frustrated.

Far too often, a casually spoken word has distracted, wounded, or prompted an ill chosen path. Every interaction we have with others can either build them up or push them down. Since none of us know how many days or years we have on this earth, let's use our remaining time to be builder-uppers.

"The people who are lifting the world onward and upward are those who encourage more than they criticize."
Elizabeth Harrison

LAUGH
OFTEN

The Reader's Digest has been suggesting it for years: laughter can be good medicine. Dr. Lee Berk of Loma Linda University Medical School found that laughter actually boosts human immunity to ward off stress-related illnesses.

Using a catheter to draw blood from the arms of healthy men while they watched a funny video, Dr. Berk compared samples with blood drawn the next day. He found that laughter had activated T lymphocytes and natural killer cells that fight infection. As a result, some hospitals and clinics have opened "humor rooms" with funny posters, books, magazines, and with light-hearted TV programming running 24 hours a day.

Business consultants remind us that humor solidifies a group, if we don't exclude or put others down with it. For a job that's repetitive or boring, laughter can also improve productivity. And it's a great way to neutralize emotionally charged events.

Laughter is helpful at home, too. In his book, *Raising Responsible Kids,* Jay Kesler, former President of Taylor University, shares the wisdom of using the light touch. When one of his children was going through a trial, Kesler would sometimes tell a funny story of himself in similar circumstances to give his teenager confidence that the problem was not unique and that things could eventually be resolved.

Laughter is pleasurable. It temporarily puts thoughts of anger and fear out of our minds, freeing us to be lighthearted, carefree, and hopeful.

If you want to fall in love with your future, try following the advice of Dr. Joel Goldman and put at least five good opportunities to laugh into each day.

"Humor lets off some of the steam in the pressure cooker of life."
Jay Kesler

CHOOSE WISELY, SEEK GOOD COUNSEL

One of our greatest personal freedoms is the power to choose. We can choose our attitudes and our habits as well as what we read, what we learn, and what we do about the future.

We're sometimes indecisive because we're waiting for the perfect moment, the perfect inspiration, or the perfect plan. But perfectionism can be deadly. Hopes and dreams may atrophy with our energy if we wait for everything to be exactly right. However, decisions don't need to be made by the flip of a coin or by the mood we're in, either. Sometimes the best help is a wise mentor.

Fighter pilot and author Doug Sherman says we have an Almighty Counselor who longs to partner with us in the process of making decisions. Each of us is extremely important to the Creator of the universe and He cares considerably about the impact of our life's work. Much like a father does.

We all know the fervent desire of most parents is to help their children make good decisions and find the best use of their talents. Often, the highest compliment a son or daughter can pay a parent is to say, "Dad, Mom, can I get your advice?" God loves being asked that, too. And unlike earthly parents, He's not capable of making mistakes.

Jim Rohn says, "Asking is the beginning of receiving." For wise choices through-out the course of life, we need to:

- stop playing the lone ranger,
- ask the best mentors we know,
- run all advice through the pool of common sense, and above all
- seek God's help.

"Decisions shape lives and good choices enable the future."

DO THE RIGHT THING

T he story is told of two elderly women walking through a country cemetery, remarking on the scenery and the tombstones. The first woman read an inscription out loud: "Here lies a politician and an honest man." "Good gracious," said the other. "Isn't it awful that they had to put two people in the same grave!"

While this amusing anecdote does not reflect fairly on the many men and women in elected positions who lead with integrity, we have all known people in various walks of life who were not what they appeared to be. People who worked harder on image than on integrity. It's actually easy to fall into that way of thinking. Commercials tell us image is everything. Online social networking subtly promotes appearance over substance. And our culture encourages the assertion of rights, but seems to ignore personal responsibility.

However, in the business world, in the community, and in relationships, it's still character that counts. Author and management consultant, Dianna Booher, advises her clients to entertain only ethical choices. Pressures do rise and temptations come. So it's smart to decide early that you will:

- never misrepresent policy,
- never pass someone else's work off as yours,
- never lie to cover your mistakes,
- always provide the best possible service,
- always keep your word on a commitment, and
- always deal honestly and fairly.

If you want to really fall in love with your future, do the right thing all the time. Integrity will give you peace of mind and an interesting byproduct—great influence in the lives of others. As Will Rogers said, "admirable behavior changes people's minds and hearts far more effectively than argument."

"When wealth is lost, nothing is lost; when health is lost, something is lost; when character is lost, all is lost."

LOOK FOR
REWARD IN
THE WORK,
NOT
IN THE PAY

In 1952, John Hetrick was driving home with his son. He'd just cleared a bend in the road when a small boulder appeared in the center of his lane. He hammered the brakes and instinctively flung a protective arm in his son's direction. With some off-road skidding, they avoided disaster. But the frightening incident stirred Hetrick's creativity.

Was it possible—in the event of a crash—to have some cushiony protection *inside* a car to shield passengers from being hit by glass and metal? As an industrial engineering technician, he went to work on his idea. A year later, he'd created the world's first air bag. It was called a "safety cushion assembly for motor vehicles."

Within forty years, 90% of American automobiles were manufactured with at least a driver's side air bag. John Hetrick, however, never made a penny from his invention. His patent expired in 1970, four years before GM introduced airbags.

Hetrick feels he's been rewarded anyway. Since airbags became available, experts say the devices save an inestimable number of people from serious injury or death every year.

Hetrick has the same belief that Thomas Edison had—that the monetary value of an invention is not its greatest reward. The reward is in the creative work, the striving to bring a dream to reality, and in the benefit it brings others.

"The reward of a thing well done is to have done it."
Ralph Waldo Emerson

WALK IN GRATITUDE

A man tells of his heartbreaking grief at the death of his 9 year old son. One day, after he had lamented the loss to a friend, she said quietly, "I never had a son." Her comment was not intended to diminish his wrenching grief, but he says that moment was like finding a rainbow in the midst of a personal storm. His son was gone, but no one could take away his joy over getting to parent that unique little boy for 9 years. Gratitude removed some of the sting of his loss.

In *A Better Way to Live*, author Og Mandino challenges his readers to look beyond discouragements and personal storms by focusing on the blessings they do have. He writes: "What's your freedom worth? How about your education or opportunities? How much would you take to give them up? . . . Would you take a million dollars for your eyes? How about your hands or feet?" His questions stimulate us to notice the multitude of true blessings we each have in our lives.

Melody Beattie comments: "Gratitude unlocks the fullness of life. It turns what we have into enough and more...It can turn a meal into a feast, a house into a home."

U.S. Labor Department statistics in 2006 indicated that 46% of those who quit their jobs in the previous year had done so because they felt unappreciated. 46%! That's why smart managers try to cultivate the habit of looking for what people do right and then expressing their appreciation specifically, personally, and positively. Gratitude motivates! Dr. Christine Northrup says gratitude "actually attracts more of the things you appreciate and value into your life."

So take the sting out of your heartaches and open yourself to the fullness of your future by facing each day with gratitude.

"I must stop focusing on what's lacking in my life and bring my complete attention to all I have—the simple abundance that surrounds us all. Small acts of kindness heal even the deepest wounds; savoring fleeting moments of comfort restores serenity."
Sarah Ban Breathnach

STRENGTHEN FAMILY RELATIONSHIPS

One great way to fall in love with your future is to work on strengthening your most important relationships—those at home. The happiest business men and women we know are the ones who are intentional about saving energy for their family members at the end of each day. And the wisest among them pray before walking in the door at night that they will be sensitive to each person's needs.

No one on his deathbed ever wishes he'd spent more time at the office. But all are glad for the time they spent investing in others and building closeness at home. The family is still the social relationship that can most give us a sense of completeness in the midst of a fragmented world.

We live in a culture that is careful about competition, but careless about human value. The human psyche needs rest from this in a home where there is thoughtfulness, encouragement, and respect. To achieve this, Ivan Panin says, "The husband needs to be blind at times; the wife, deaf; and both need, much of the time, to be dumb." Overlooking each other's faults is wise counsel.

In tough times, warmth at home gives perspective for today and hope for the future. Perhaps that's why marriage counselor Gary Smalley advises that we get our "strokes" at home. If we live so that our greatest affirmations come from family members rather than business associates, we're enriching our private lives and the lives of our family members.

"The happiest moments in my life have been those which I have passed at home in the comfort of my family."
Thomas Jefferson

CULTIVATE
FRIENDSHIPS

For years, we've been watching technology change the work force, often wondering how it will affect our personal value, productivity, and economic security. Computer software, indeed, becomes more amazing all the time. However, machines can't listen when we need a sounding board, support us through a crisis, or offer a warm hug.

Dan Sullivan, author of *The 21rst Century Agent*, claims that no matter how fast and powerful the microchip becomes, it will never replace certain uniquely human capabilities. One is the ability to go beyond mere "networking" and build meaningful human relationships.

Whether in the Board room or at home, friendships empower and heal. In fact, clinical studies show that people under intense emotional stress tend to have a death rate two to three times higher than those with calmer lives—unless the stressee has a dependable web of intimate friends. Then there is little relationship between stress and early death.

We develop these important emotional networks by:

- finding things in common with others,
- showing interest in their lives,
- celebrating their victories,
- doing favors,
- being transparent about ourselves, and
- showing people we need them by occasionally asking for help.

People in love with their future cherish their connection with friends and family members. They value the unique characteristics of each friend, even as they are appreciating the intellectual stimulation and emotional support. We add rich blessing to the future when we honor and cultivate relationships.

"If we had to name what makes life worth living, most of us would say it's the people we love: relationships make the difference in the quality of life at all ages."
Richard J. Leider

LEARN THE EXHILARATION OF SERVING

Kindness cures. In fact, medical physician Dr. William McGath claimed that 90% of all mental illness could have been prevented or cured by ordinary kindness. Realizing this, he tried to be sure he never ended a day without extending at least one unexpected kindness to someone. When possible, he did this anonymously, because he didn't want the focus to be on him—he just wanted to bless another person.

In a similar vein, experts tell us not to look for appreciation or thanks for our labor. The effect of thoughtful service is often subtle, and the best reward might be the inner joy of knowing we did a good thing and did it well. However, we should savor those occasional serendipitous moments when we *do* see the fruit of our labor or receive a word of appreciation.

One Saturday last fall, our daughter and several friends spontaneously decided to surprise an elderly neighbor by raking and bagging the leaves in her tree-laden yard. When the neighbor discovered who her anonymous gardeners were, she called with thankful tears in her voice, saying she'd been very worried about how she was going to rake the leaves following her surgery. She felt this service was God's answer to her prayers. The girls had not expected thanks, but they savored those heartfelt words.

Emmett Fox once said, "If you could only love enough, you'd be the most powerful person in the world." There is great power in treating others with honor, love, and respect. Actually, loving service—given freely—offers a picture of the grace of God; it's a priceless gift that can never be repaid.

If we want to have a legacy we'll always be proud of, service to others is the key. Because, the truth is, we achieve our dreams when we help others achieve their dreams.

"Join the company of those who make the barren places of life fruitful with kindness."
Helen Keller

DON'T ASSUME
ONLY THE
YOUNG
CAN LOOK TO
THE FUTURE

U ntil the moment of death, we each have potential and we have a future. Though no one can go back and start over, anyone can start now and have a brand new future. The future stretches before us like soft freshly poured cement, waiting for the imprint we give it by our habits and our choices.

History abounds with examples of people who began their most significant contribution later in life. Perhaps it's because people with more years under their belts have a larger network of associates and a deeper pool of past mistakes to help them better assess a new project. Additionally, human nature sometimes values the future more when there is less of it. Maturity can also give us the ability to get very intentional about a project, perhaps making an impact in fewer years.

A by-product of "future excitement" for people of all ages is that we tend to stay healthier, live longer, and fend off disease better when we have a purpose greater than ourselves to get up for each morning.

Successful businessman John O. Todd was still creating 10, 15, and 20 year plans for himself when he was 75 years old. He realized each of those dreams and lived vibrantly into his 90's.

One advantage of age is that we are no longer drawn to the hurried pace of youth or middle age. We see the value of working toward goals at a reasonable rate, and we give ourselves the luxury of slowing down to do things that will renew us—like playing with our grandchildren. Many say the later decades of life may be our best: we can enjoy learning as if we would live forever, and we can enjoy loving as if we might die tomorrow.

"No matter what your age, tomorrow is the first day of the rest of life."

CONSIDER YOUR ULTIMATE FUTURE

With chemical and nuclear weapons widespread today, with serious financial crises facing our nation, and with natural disasters taking their toll, we sometimes wonder if we will be robbed of our future—or if our children and grandchildren will.

But alarming political, economic and natural disasters aren't the only threats to our future. Personal heartaches like cancer, the loss of a job, or the death of someone we love can make the future look bleak—the future in this world. However, our greatest future is yet to come.

At the center of this new future is a person the world might call a Turnaround Specialist. Many rate him the best CEO the world has ever known. In describing this manager's style, noted author and business consultant Laurie Beth Jones says, "If you trace the results of his energy…, everything bloomed, was healed, or came to life in his presence." He's unique in that his awesome results are never at the expense of individuals. He's a servant leader who cares deeply about each person and invites all to call him by his first name…Jesus.

When He reverses one of our losses or miraculously brings peace into the depth of a personal sorrow, He's demonstrating small glimpses of what Heaven will be like in His Father's presence—wrongs will be righted, hurts healed, and intimacy restored. Joy will be boundless in every way imaginable! Jesus invites *all* to know Him, learn His ways, and come under His leadership. Those who accept His offer can look forward to the future for which we were all created—an eternal face-to-face relationship with the Specialist of our souls.

When we receive and embrace this magnificent future, we begin to see how temporary our current challenges are, and we can more easily focus on maximizing the time and talents God has given us for this short life.

"My religious belief teaches me to feel as safe in battle as in bed. God has fixed the time for my death. I do not concern myself about that, except to always be ready, no matter when it may overtake me."
General Stonewall Jackson

MAKE A DIFFERENCE
DEVELOP A VISION THAT FITS YOU
LOOK WHERE YOU WANT TO GO
STRETCH YOURSELF NOW TO SOAR LATER
THINK FEEDBACK NOT FAILURE
ENJOY THE REWARDS OF PLANNING
DON'T LET DISASTER KEEP YOU DOWN
EXERCISE PERSONAL POWER
WORK ON YOUR BEST RESOURCE: YOUR BODY
RECOGNIZE THE POWER OF WORDS
LAUGH OFTEN
CHOOSE WISELY; SEEK GOOD COUNSEL
DO THE RIGHT THING
LOOK FOR REWARD IN THE WORK,
NOT THE PAY
WALK IN GRATITUDE
STRENGTHEN FAMILY RELATIONSHIPS
CULTIVATE FRIENDSHIPS
LEARN THE EXHILARATION OF SERVING
DON'T ASSUME ONLY THE YOUNG
HAVE A FUTURE
CONSIDER YOUR ULTIMATE FUTURE

W illiam James said, "The greatest use of each day is to spend it for something that outlasts it"—to live a meaningful life and use your full potential, despite personal circumstances.

Though no one can start over, anyone can start today and have a brand new finish, going beyond survival and beyond success to pursue a significant purpose with passion.

The process of falling in love with your future is exciting, because each person's future is as unique as his/her own fingerprint. And everyone's destiny will have a different impact on the world.

For most people, getting passionate about the future will likely include the following principles:

1. Make a realistic assessment of your God-given worth and talents. Then determine the responsibilities they carry and the habits that may need to be broken to live out the destiny for which you were born.

2. Understand that the effect of all actions is cumulative, not immediate. So read good books, choose heroic models, associate with virtuous people, and train yourself to do what is honorable and nutritious.

3. Spend energy on relationships before tasks and on what you want to accomplish rather than what you want to avoid. The most powerful legacies are built on relationships and visions...and then on servitude. Usually you'll achieve your dreams as you help others achieve their dreams.

"Tomorrow is the first day of the rest of your life. A destiny awaits your decisions. You are invited to discover passion for your potential and fall in love with your future."

ABOUT THE AUTHORS

Helping people be the best they can be is **Ron Beshear**'s passion. As a high school teacher and coach, he led his forensics and tennis teams to state championships. Later his love for helping people pursue their dreams influenced him to join the financial services industry, where he could help families chart a course to strengthen their finances for the future.

His business career includes serving 22 years as the Managing Partner of a financial services network and as the CEO of an employee benefits company. While heading these firms, he also served as the franchise operator of a retail store, and the branch manager of an investment firm.

In the civic arena, Ron was a Founding Board Member of Cincinnati Hills Christian Academy, and he currently serves on numerous Trustee Boards in Cincinnati and Northern Kentucky. Additionally he is a popular speaker and Master of Ceremonies at national fundraising banquets and special events.

In her writing, teaching, and mentoring, **Mary Beshear** shares Ron's love of encouragement. As a high school teacher, Mary enjoyed helping teens learn the skills of critical thinking, creative writing, and confident public speaking.

After earning a PhD at Marquette University, she turned her career energies to homemaking and parenting. On the side, she wrote scripts for radio, edited a pastor's sermons, taught women's Bible studies, and did feature writing for a national magazine. She has written two books in addition to this publication: *The One HE loves,* an inspirational Bible Study for women, and *Fight the Good Fight,* the true story of a mother's legacy.

Over the years, Mary has served on Trustee Boards for her church, for her children's school, and for numerous nonprofit organizations in Cincinnati. She says her favorite roles involve being a wife to Ron, a mother to Ben and Robin, a mother-in-law to Lindsey, and a grandmother to Logan.

For more information on Ron and Mary, visit **www.servingyourpurpose.com**

One of life's sweet blessings is celebrating with others the gifts and surprises God brings our way. If this book has given you any additional traction in pursuing your unique destiny, we would love to hear your anecdotes and success stories. Please feel free to contact us at www.servingyourpurpose.com.

Made in the USA
Charleston, SC
17 May 2014